I Like Biographies!

Read About
Annie Oakley

Stephen Feinstein

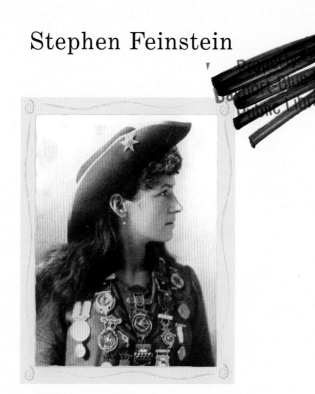

Enslow Elementary

an imprint of

Enslow Publishers, Inc.

40 Industrial Road	PO Box 38
Box 398	Aldershot
Berkeley Heights, NJ 07922	Hants GU12 6BP
USA	UK

http://www.enslow.com

Words to Know

pigeon (PIH-jun)—A kind of bird.

pioneer (PIE-uh-neer)—A person who is one of the first to explore and settle a place.

rifle (RIE-ful)—A kind of long gun.

sharpshooter (SHARP-shoo-ter)—Someone who is very good at shooting guns at targets.

Enslow Elementary, an imprint of Enslow Publishers, Inc.

Enslow Elementary® is a registered trademark of Enslow Publishers, Inc.

Library of Congress Cataloging-in-Publication Data

Feinstein, Stephen.
  Read about Annie Oakley / Stephen Feinstein.
    p. cm. — (I like biographies!)
  Includes bibliographical references and index.
  ISBN 0-7660-2583-7
  1. Oakley, Annie, 1860–1926—Juvenile literature.
2. Shooters of firearms—United States—Biography—
Juvenile literature. 3. Entertainers—United States—
Biography—Juvenile literature. 4. Women entertainers—
United States—Biography—Juvenile literature. I. Title.
II. Series.
GV1157.O3F45 2006
799.3'092—dc22
  [B]
                    2005016431

Printed in the United States of America

10 9 8 7 6 5 4 3 2 1

To Our Readers: We have done our best to make sure all Internet Addresses in this book were active and appropriate when we went to press. However, the author and the publisher have no control over and assume no liability for the material available on those Internet sites or on links to other Web sites. Any comments or suggestions can be sent by e-mail to comments@enslow.com or to the address on the back cover.

Every effort has been made to locate all copyright holders of material used in this book. If any errors or omissions have occurred, corrections will be made in future editions of this book.

Illustration Credits: All photos are from the The Darke County Historical Society, Inc., except as follows: Denver Public Library, Western History Collection, #NS-245, p. 22; Dover Publications, pp. 13, 19; Ohio Historical Society, pp. 15, 17.

Cover Illustration: The Darke County Historical Society, Inc.

Contents

Chapter 1

Growing Up in a Log Cabin

Annie Oakley was born in Ohio on August 13, 1860. Her real name was Phoebe Ann Mosey. Her parents, Jacob and Susan, were **pioneers**. They lived in a log cabin in the woods.

Annie's father hunted small animals to feed the family. Annie liked to walk in the woods with her father. He showed her how to set traps to catch animals.

Phoebe Ann Mosey grew up to become Annie Oakley, a famous sharpshooter.

One winter day when Annie was five, Jacob got caught in a snowstorm. By the time he got home, his hands were frozen and he could not speak. Jacob died several weeks later.

Annie and her sisters and brothers worked hard to help their mother. They cooked, cleaned, sewed, and worked in the garden. But there was often not enough food.

Annie's mother (shown here) had to earn money to feed her seven children. She worked at nearby farms taking care of babies.

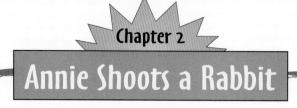
When Annie was seven, she brought food to the table. She set traps and caught a few small animals. But the family was still hungry sometimes.

One day, Annie went into the woods with her father's **rifle**. She saw a rabbit and aimed at it. She fired the rifle. There was a loud crack. The gun sprang back and hit Annie in the nose! But she had hit the rabbit with her first shot.

This picture shows how Annie dressed to go hunting.

When Annie was ten, her mother could no longer feed all the children. She sent Annie to live in a home for poor people. A farmer hired Annie to help out with chores. He and his wife were mean. Sometimes they beat Annie. When she was twelve, Annie ran away. She went back to the home for poor people. Later she moved back with her family.

This is the house Annie lived in with her family.

After Annie moved back home, she went hunting in the woods every day. She became skilled at shooting animals on the move. She shot rabbits, squirrels, and wild turkeys. She gave some of the meat to her family and sold some of it to stores in town.

Annie was proud that she could get food for her family.

13

One day Annie entered a shooting contest against Frank Butler, a famous **sharpshooter**. Annie hit twenty-three **pigeons**. Frank hit only twenty-one. Frank was so amazed by Annie's skill with a rifle that he fell in love with her. Frank sent love poems to Annie and won her heart. When Annie turned sixteen, she and Frank got married.

Frank Butler was surprised to be beaten by a fifteen-year-old girl.

15

Annie and Frank put together a traveling shooting act called Butler and Oakley. (No one knows why Annie took the name "Oakley." One story says that it was the name of the town where she met Frank.) Wherever Annie and Frank went, people were thrilled by Annie's shooting.

This poster shows Annie and Frank with their dog, George. He was part of their act, too.

BUTLER & OAKLEY

In 1885, Annie joined a show called Buffalo Bill's Wild West. The show traveled all over the world. Annie became famous. She took all kinds of trick shots and never missed her targets.

The cowboys and Indians in the show loved Annie. When Chief Sitting Bull saw what Annie could do with a gun, he named her "Little Sure Shot."

Buffalo Bill's real name was William Cody. He and Chief Sitting Bull (on the right) were good friends with Annie.

19

In 1901, Annie was hurt in a train crash. She had to stop performing in the Wild West show.

Annie spent the rest of her life helping people in need, especially children. She also gave shooting lessons to thousands of women. Annie kept her "sure shot" until her death on November 3, 1926.

Even after the accident, Annie was able to ride and shoot. Here she is with her horse, Highball.

21

Timeline

1860—Annie Oakley (Phoebe Ann Mosey) is born on August 13.

1866—Annie's father, Jacob Mosey, dies.

1870—Annie goes to live at a home for poor people.

1876—Annie marries Frank Butler on August 23.

1885—Annie joins Buffalo Bill's Wild West show.

1901—Annie is hurt in a train accident.

1926—Annie Oakley dies on November 3.

Learn More

Books

Gibbons, Gail. *Yippee-yay! A Book About Cowboys and Cowgirls*. Boston: Little, Brown, 1998.

Landau, Elaine. *Annie Oakley: Wild West Sharpshooter*. Berkeley Heights, N.J.: Enslow Publishers, Inc., 2004.

Silate, Jennifer. *Little Sure Shot: Annie Oakley and Buffalo Bill's Wild West Show*. New York: Rosen, 2004.

Web Sites

Women in History: Annie Oakley

<http://www.lkwdpl.org/wiohio/oakl-ann.htm>

Annie Oakley: A Dorchester Library Profile

<http://www.dorchesterlibrary.org/library/oakley.html>

Index